AF499342

ACKNOWLEDGEMENTS

I would like to acknowledge first and foremost my creator who had gifted me with the skills of writing and my love and passion to create. As someone who has lost sight of her faith time and time again, it is an encouraging thought to know that no matter how far I wander, He is always there to set me back on track. This project would not have been possible to complete or near to publishing had it not been for Mr. Simpson and his team at Good News Jamaica. It is honestly a dream come true and heartwarming to have had him and his team in my corner, patiently waiting for me to complete this project and granting me the opportunity of a lifetime. I am also grateful to my friends, family and friends who became family, who encouraged me and never stopped pushing me to be the best person I could be.

I probably would have given up writing but thanks to their constant nagging, I never did, and I am able to share my talent beyond my inner circle. Finally, this book is centered around growth, so it is only fair to acknowledge and thank myself for never giving up and pushing through the many obstacles that were made to break me, but instead, built me. It has presented the opportunity to speak to my younger self and to assist younger individuals in gaining some level of understanding of life.

DEAR YOUNGER ME: THINGS I WISH I KNEW

Copyright © 2022 by Danielle Tavares

All Rights Reserved.

Thank you for purchasing an authorized edition of this book and for complying with copyright laws by not reproducing, scanning, or distributing any part of it in any form without permission.

TABLE OF CONTENT

September 2008

There are many things you will not be able to control.

> You will not be able to control the actions of others.
>
> You will not be able to control others' perception of you.
>
> You will not be able to control how others interpret your words and actions.

Do not allow what you cannot control to consume you.

Do not allow them to steal your joy.

December 2008

You are still worthy.

You will feel tempted to go out and try new things.

You will feel tempted to go with the crowd and for a split second, you may lose sight of who you are, your beliefs, your own thoughts - you may lose yourself.

You will wander aimlessly, and you will gravitate to the first sign of comfort, even if it is not good. I need you to understand that no matter how far you wander and what you do, you are not defined by it.

You are still worthy.

March 2009

You will want to speak
The words will be buried beneath your fear of never being understood

You will want to scream
The sound will be lodged in your throat, strangled by your fear of never being heard

You will want to cry
The scalding tears will sting your eyes, but never once will they fall, stopped by the fear of being perceived as weak

You will want to disappear
The urge will be stopped by the fear of being a coward, forever running

That is all it will take you to bury yourself deeper -
Fear.

June 2009

You will not be perfect.

Sometimes you will mess up.

Sometimes you will say or do the wrong thing.

Sometimes you will lose your temper.

Sometimes patience will not be your best virtue.

Sometimes you will look into the mirror and highlight your ‘flaws’.

Sometimes you will not have that soft, timid laugh.

Sometimes you will cry because it will get too much.

Sometimes you will be Human,

What you will learn is that your imperfections are what make you perfect.

September 2009

You will not be defined by your insecurities

You will not be defined by your weight

You will not be defined by your height

You will not be defined by your body size

You will not be defined by your grades

You will not be defined by your mental health

You will not be defined by your disability

You will not be defined by your society

-- You will be defined by your creator

The apologies that heal us
do not come from others who have hurt us,
but rather the apologies that come from us hurting ourselves.

December 2009

Do not be afraid of growth and do not be afraid of knowledge.

The truth is you will never stop growing.

> You are you but as you grow, you will become combined fragments of the people you will meet, the books you will read, the songs you will have listened to, the places you will visit, the random facts you will have stumbled upon, the pieces that you create and all the people you will come to love.

You will come to learn that you do not lose yourself along the way but that instead, you will have created yourself.

Every bit of you will be an extension of who you would have been yesterday.

March 2010

The world will give you every reason to leave, yet you will choose to stay.

The world intends to tear you apart, yet you will hold yourself together.

You will encounter darkness, yet you will choose light.

You will choose to radiate kindness because you will know the harshness of the world.

Softness will choose your words as you will have come to know the weight that they carry.

You will choose to stand firm, even when the world beats you to the ground, you will rise.

Your very existence is defiance.

June 2010

Never forget Sweetheart - life will be about the little things.

Feel the excitement as the train passes by.

Embrace the beauty of the sunset.

Feel the thrill of rewatching your favorite movie.

Go crazy experimenting with a new recipe.

Bask in the warmth of the sun on your walk home.

Enjoy the salty taste of your tears when your favorite character dies.

Do not waste your days waiting for something big to happen.

Take life by the reins and enjoy every moment of the ride.

September 2010

You will stare in the mirror, and you will question, *"What do they see?"* I hope that one day you will grow to learn that beauty is only skin deep.

You see bland, brown eyes
They see flecks of gold that dance with the sun's rays
You see a crooked smile
They see the source of light, by the way your smile lights up the room
You see a darker complexion
They see where the sun has kissed
You see imperfections
They see your heart

They will have experienced your soul and to them, you are perfect.

December 2010

It will be you.

It will be you who will have so much pressure around you.

So many voices will tell you what to do, who you should be, and these voices will drown out your own.

You will be left confused and full of fear of disappointing all these voices.

One day you will be able to see: you will learn that no matter how hard you try, no matter how much you fake it, you cannot be anyone else but yourself.

You will smile and walk with your head held high.

You will smile because you will not have found yourself, but you will be creating yourself.

You will be learning who you are.

Forget those who will be disappointed because Sweetheart, not everyone is going to like you.

The ones who matter are the ones who allow you to be you.

Be authentic and unapologetic about it.

And what if,
Expressing your emotions
Is what makes you
Strong,
And concealing your emotions
Is what makes you
Weak?

March 2011

If there is one thing, I wish I knew before, it would be to just love yourself.

I know it may be overstated but Darling, it's true.

When everyone leaves, the only person that can't leave you, is you.

You are the only person that will be around yourself for the rest of your life 24/7.

You will be compelled to learn about your quirks and to love your flaws regardless of your feelings.

You will grow with yourself until the last breath you take.

The least you can do for you, is love yourself.

June 2011

It will be you

You will be afraid of getting better

Your soul will become so attached to your sadness that it will become your safety zone.

The thought of getting better and healing from your trauma will scare you: terrify you even.

Your personality will form from the security you will find in not being okay and the thought of being okay will be beyond what you can see.

It will raise warning bells in your mind that you will be entering uncharted territories, then you will find yourself retreating in your shell terrified.

Terrified of the unknown.

Terrified of being better.

September 2011

You are mistaken if you think you are so easily forgotten.

Your smile is one to remember for years.

Your beautiful, brown eyes hold the power to captivate.

Your melodious laughter resonates throughout the room, and everyone cannot help but to stop and behold everything that is your beauty.

Your smart mouth and intelligence are one for the books.

Your kindness and compassion compel others to gravitate towards you with ease and

even when you are gone, you will never be gone.

Your legacy will live in their minds and be carried to their children.

Do not think that no one cares because my dear, you are mistaken if you think you are so easily forgotten.

December 2011

And Sweetheart, do not allow them to place you into a box.

Do not allow them to pin you down by their expectations of who they think you should be, where they think you should go, what they think you should believe.

My Dear, you were never meant to be confined by the expectations of those around you.

You were meant to outgrow the version of yourself that you were yesterday.

You were never meant to be confined by the version of you that they created in their minds.

You were meant to spread your wings to enter into this world and make mistakes to learn.

You were meant to find your place in the world and not in the box they placed you in.

March 2012

It can be discouraging when all you pray for is peace but instead, you often find yourself being thrown into a storm. You are left dazed, confused, fearful and you feel betrayed.

> *Did my request fall on deaf ears?*
> *Does God not think I have had enough?*
> *Is He even listening?*

I will not lie to you and say that your faith will not waver because it will waver - perhaps more than it should. In the middle of the storm Sweetheart, close your eyes and comfort yourself in the thought of a promising future. *Your* future. You may wonder how it is that you can think about something that was not even promised to us. That my dear is the act of Faith.

As you give parts of yourself away to everyone else,
do not forget to save
a part of yourself for you too.

June 2012

The thought of being different scares people.

Beauty scares people.

The beauty of being different scares people.

> You will be expected to put on a performance of who fakes normalcy the best because not many will want to love your mental illness. Not many will love your physical disability. Not many will view you worthy enough if you do not fit the narrative of normalcy. Very few will show you that you are worthy of love, and they will show you the beauty in being different.

You will have to learn to decipher if you will want to believe the few or subscribe to the many.

September 2012

Nothing will feel wrong, but it will not feel right either.

Your mind is an oddly calm haze.

Your anxiety will rage in your mind, clawing at the cage, willing for your thoughts to roam free. The words will be there until they are not.

You will feel, but you won't.

You will want to speak but you can't.

You will not say what is on your mind, afraid to unleash the destructive thoughts that live there rent free.

You can imagine it as slightly cracking the door open but then it will be out of your control when everything comes tumbling through.

December 2012

Life will be funny in many ways.

While the conscious parts of your brain will erase people, you will never truly lose or forget someone because in the time frame you would have known them - no matter how short - they will cause you to think twice.

Subconsciously, they will become a part of you.

You may adopt a mannerism from them.

If they wrong you, they will make you wiser.

They may change your perspective on a particular subject matter.

These will be versions of an invisible tattoo.

We will all be connected in some way because that person will change who you are - for better or for worse - even in the slightest way.

Chances are, you may indirectly meet them through another.

Consider that everyone will be connected through a chain reaction.

March 2013

You will hope for Peace, Happiness, Success, a Family, your Dream Job, or even Financial Stability.

Only time will tell - know this -

One thing that will be guaranteed in Life is Death

You will never know when

It will crawl underneath your door like the smoke lingering to infect your lungs

Or it will creep upon you like a thief in the night

You will never know when it is going to come

Embrace the life you will have

Rather than Fearing the Inevitable

June 2013

There is a part of healing that they will not tell you about.

It is the part where even when you're happy, you will still long for the sadness.

You will long to see the world from a realistic point of view.

You will long to feel nothing.

My Darling, I assure you that there is nothing wrong with you.

You will merely have made the sadness your home and you will wander away.

You will spread your wings and leave it behind with no intentions of returning.

It will be okay to feel a little homesick, but I hope one day, you will be able to make your happiness your new home.

You will never be behind.
While everyone else is focused on elevating,
You will be focused on surviving
And you will.
Then it will be your time to live.

September 2013

Change is good. Change is okay.

You will not have to fear change because you will come to realize that overtime, you too will change.

You will unlearn the toxic behaviors from your childhood, you will realize that not everyone deserves to have access to you, and you will develop boundaries.

You will learn more and more about yourself as the years pass by and your opinions will change once you know better.

You will have developed a mind of your own and that will require you to break free and be your own person.

Embrace that individuality.

Change may feel scary, but I assure you Sweetheart, it is necessary, and it is okay.

Embrace the changes you will face for it is inescapable.

You either fear change or make change fear you.

December 2013

When you are healing, a part of you will always mourn.

It will mourn for the person for the person you were.

It will mourn for all the opportunities you miss because of pain.

It will mourn for the dark days.

It will mourn for the unseen smiles and unheard laughter.

It will mourn for what you think you will deserve and what you will accept when you are at your lowest.

When the rain clouds disappear and the sunshine starts to make itself at home, allow yourself to feel. Allow yourself to mourn for the person you would have left behind.

March 2014

And then suddenly, one day, you will break.
You will be broken into tiny pieces, shattered.
They will have killed your inner child and then
suddenly, it will be dark.
There will seem to be no light at the end of the tunnel,
the sun or moon will not shine like once upon a time,
your coffee will be bland, your passion dissolved, and
you will merely exist in the shelf of yourself.
All the tiny moments meant to break you will have
finally caught up to you and you will feel alone.
You will feel dejected, and you will feel that you are
at the end but Sweetheart, you are not. You will
merely be approaching the beginning.
You will look the storm in the eye, you will smile,
they will cower, and you will be victorious.

June 2014

Do not pay any mind to what they will say for they can never be pleased.

If you are too insecure, you will be told you are only doing it to gain compliments and validation, because you should already be aware of your beauty.

Dare you acknowledge your beauty and suddenly you will be thought to be vain and conceited. Little will they know how long it will take you to look beyond your insecurities.

Little will they know how many times you will find yourself weighing yourself on a scale. Little will they know how many times you will eat too much or eat too little.

Little will they know.

So again, I say Darling, they will never be pleased so live how you deem fit.

September 2014

Appreciate the sadness.

There will be this pressure to always be happy, but life is not all rainbows and sunshine.

Life is also thunderstorms, showers, hurricanes, tsunamis, volcanoes, and earthquakes.

There will be moments in life that will tear you apart and make you want to leave.

You will be allowed to grieve and cry, scream if you must.

Do not be pressured to believe you have to be happy all the time and place a lid on the negative feelings.

These moments that break you will help you to appreciate more the moments that will mend and build you.

The sadness, anger, pain, and frustration will make you appreciate the contentment and joy more.

Soon, you will find yourself being appreciative of them all - the good and the bad.

You deserve a wholesome type of love.
Do not settle for someone who only loves you piece by piece.

December 2014

You have such a pure soul.

The kind that wants to save everyone around you.

You feel so deeply that even the people with the hardest shells melt around you.

You will be the safe space for so many and you will hold them up but sometimes, the pressure will begin to break you.

You will start to feel yourself slipping beyond the surface.

This is where you will have to choose Sweetheart.

Will you save everyone else while you are drowning, or will you finally come to realize that it is okay to choose yourself too?

March 2015

There is always going to be a cloud that hovers over your head, shadowing every movement you make.

The darkness it will carry will feel all too familiar.

You will feel yourself being lured and tempted to return to it.

I always thought that you had to fight it - that the only way to win was to resist.

Little did I know that I was only fueling it.

You will learn one day to become one with it - accept it.

Then you pray to God that you will not lose yourself again.

June 2015

As you grow, you will come to understand the distinction between a *want* and a *need.*

You want someone like those in the movies you binge or the novels you stay up all night reading.

You want a person who is willing to kill themselves if it means saving you.

Someone who would do everything to prove to you that they are willing to break, just to match your brokenness.

Someone who brings thunderstorms and lightning.

What if the person you want is not the person you need?

What if all you need is someone whole?

Someone who is willing to help you in your own healing journey.

Someone who would fight tooth and nail to help glue your pieces back together, even when they know you would never be whole again.

They would know you have some cracked bits but will love and care for you regardless.

What if all you need is someone who brings the sunshine with a little light rain?

September 2015

The things you once knew to be simple will become complex.

You will never view the world in black and white, but rather an array of colors in a beautiful, yet conflicting blend.

In time, the hero or heroine of your story will not be painted in such a perfect light, and they will exhibit traits similar to that of the villain.

Perhaps, you will find that the villain may not be as bad as you once thought.

You will find the lines between them to be blurred together - one with sharp cuts and the other with a soft touch.

You will grow to carry anger that is not yours and seek love that you cannot find within yourself in an attempt to seal the wounds inflicted upon you.

You, yourself will find you to be the most complex person you will ever live with.

While others will think that they have figured you out, you will only then just be putting your puzzle pieces together.

December 2015

You will be constantly asked about the things you love, and they will flash through your mind with ease

-- coffee, your loved ones, photography, art, sunsets, the scent of rain on hot pavement, the scent of gasoline, sunflowers, writing, animals, clothing, expressing yourself, the color yellow, the inexperienced season of autumn, smiling, hearing hearty laughter, the refreshing feeling of water on a hot, summer day, binging movies all day, reading all night, staying awake with someone knowing it will only leave you tired the following morning, singing in the shower, weddings, the beach, the serenity of waves crashing along the shore

-- but how long will it take before you mention yourself?

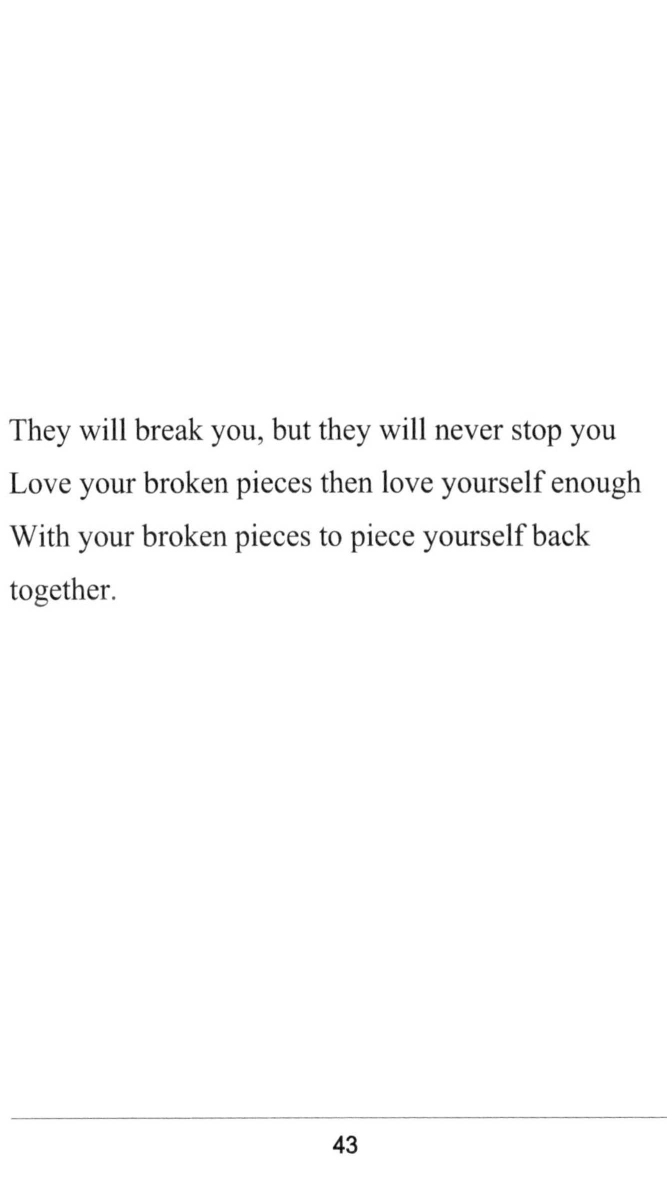

They will break you, but they will never stop you
Love your broken pieces then love yourself enough
With your broken pieces to piece yourself back
together.

March 2016

You will long for the day that you will finally fall in love again.

I do not mean falling in love with that brown-eyed boy who has a smile that will set you on a high, no.

I meant falling in love with life.

You will long for the day that waking up does not feel like a chore, you will long for the day that you do not carry a burning anger within you that will be directed at the mere fact that you are still, somehow alive.

You will long to walk with your head held high, you will long to feel like you are no longer drowning in mid-air.

You will hope to one day feel lighter and happier - when sadness will no longer dictate your life but rather make you feel more appreciative of the good.

You will no longer view the world in black and white, that you will be able to witness it in all the colors God made for us to see.

You will grow more appreciative of the little things - the rain drumming against the pavement, the leaves dancing with the wind, the sweet aroma of coffee trapped within your nostrils, the harsh sun rays that smile upon us.

You will long for the day that you can look back on your present self and be able to say, “You will make it.”

June 2016

I think the biggest misconception you will have about life is that there is a finishing line where all your worries, struggles, trauma, and pain will cease to exist.

A finishing line where you will move across, and they will cease to follow you.

I wish someone told me that the only finishing line is the one at the end of the tunnel where you meet the bright light.

All the pain you will carry is a part of your journey.

You will forever disappoint yourself trying to cross that non-existent finish line.

You will have to learn to live with the understanding that the pains and disappointments of life are a part of your journey, otherwise you will only keep disappointing yourself trying to achieve the unattainable.

September 2016

You are going to live to please them, in fear of disappointing them.

You are going to suppress who you are just for their acceptance.

You are going to place them on this pedestal and in your eyes, they could do no wrong.

As you grow, so will your maturity.

You will see glimpses of the real them, but you are going to comfort yourself in believing the version of them our 7-year-old self-painted.

You won't learn then, but you eventually will.

Manipulation will be their finest game and sadly, you will grow to be their finest player.

As you grow apart, you will think of it as you are losing them, but little will you know it will be them that lost you.

December 2016

"Carpe Diem - Seize the Day"

Learn to live and not just survive.

Take the risk and just do it.

Whatever it is, just do it.

Life is filled with so many unspoken rules that dictate our lives but what is the point of living if you are not alive?

As the poets would have it, seize the day.

Do not wait and overthink it, but rather let yourself go.

When you are older and you reflect on the life you lived, you will realize that you never truly lived but merely survived.

You will not have the satisfaction of living a full life but rather the regret of the memories you wished you made.

Instead, you will be left with a dream to turn back the hands of time and leave knowing you never could.

March 2017

You will scroll along the timeline and all you will see is what you are not.

> You are not curvy enough. You are not thick enough. You are not tall enough or perhaps; you are not short enough. Your hips are not broad enough. Your breasts are not small enough. Your bottom is not round or big enough. Your nose is not small enough.

"I am not enough," you will say. I long for the day that you realize outer beauty will only get you so far.

> The way you put others before yourself is admirable. The way you go the extra mile to ensure everyone has a smile on their face is applaudable. The way you attempt to fix others' hearts, even when your own is breaking is commendable. The way you hold everyone else up, even when you are falling apart is remarkable.

My Darling, you will be more than enough.

Choose something that makes your day, no matter how small it may be.
Let that be the reason you look forward to tomorrow.
That is how you stay.

June 2017

All your life, you will be warned about drugs.

You will have been told that they are no good for you and that they will only ruin you.

They will tell you that one drink, one sniff, is all it takes for you to be hooked.

They will never tell you about the boy with the alluring brown eyes.

They will never warn you about the intoxicating taste of his lips.

They will never warn you about the craving that will be left after his touch.

No one will warn you that he will become your addiction.

September 2017

It will be sad to witness how easy it will be to get caught up in the bait of rushing life to meet the standards of society.

You will feel that it may be 'too late' or that you would have 'never made enough' of life.

Why? Because society has labeled them in life by age.

The truth? There is never an age to what you will accomplish, and I wish I understood this.

So, what if you want to get married at 20 or 40? Do it.

So, what if you wish to achieve your degree at 30? Go for it.

Want to start over at 50? Nothing will be stopping you but you.

The only thing late in society is the memo that is never too late.

December 2017

There will be an unspoken command to cling to the version of yourself you were months ago.

You will be told how different you are acting and the version of yourself who has learnt boundaries, confidence and self-worth is a threat to those who are unable to grow with you.

You will pose a threat to those who will no longer be able to take advantage of you.

Do not be afraid of growing and accepting that the future version of yourself will not be the same as the past version of yourself.

March 2018

You will not always have the Instagram worthy photographs or the money and clothes for the best restaurants

You will not always be the one who is picked, the one who is loved the most or the one who is seen

However, my Dear,

You will always have the blurry photographs of the best memories

You will always have the love and the attention of the ones who truly matter

You will always have the warmth of the sunset, the rich scent of your morning coffee and the heart to love

June 2018

You will have those days.

Those days that are like thunderstorms.

Those days where they all will seem to be blurred into one.

Those days where you will forget the day and even the month you are in.

Those days that are routine, bland with little to no variation.

Those days that will carry a similar dull, blank feeling you carried days prior.

You will have those days.

But you will also have those days that will feel like sunshine.

Those days where you will experience joy and peace.

Those days where your coffee will taste sweeter and the sunset a bit more breathtaking.

Those days where smiling will not be a chore, but rather a gentle gesture.

Those days where you will look forward to the
next while you reminisce on those before.
Those days that would have been worth waiting for.

Watching everyone you love leave your life will grant you scars.
The deepest one that will never heal
will be the thought of wanting to leave yourself too.

September 2018

The concept of beauty is for you to define. If you do not define it for yourself, others will and very few will perceive beauty to be what it truly is.

> The patriarchy will perhaps define beauty to be women who can sit still, follow them blindly and cater to the needs of men at home.
>
> Your parents will perhaps define beauty to be intelligence shown by your accomplishments.
>
> Your partner will perhaps define beauty to be the version of you that they will create in their minds.
>
> Other women will perhaps define beauty to be what society dictates they should be.
>
> You will perhaps, for some time, define beauty to be the art of pleasing and validation.

Do not allow others to define beauty for you.

December 2018

No one will love you for you.

Do not confuse this for me saying that you will never be loved for being authentic and true to yourself.

All your quirks, your contagious laughter, your heart-stopping smile, your handcrafted curves, your self-inflicted scars from battle, your gorgeous, sad eyes - I love these things about you.

Remember Sweetheart, you must love yourself too.

Loving yourself is a task that no one else can do for you but rather something you have to do yourself.

So again, I say to you, no one can love you, for you.

March 2019

You will have to learn to walk away.

This will not be easy, especially if you wait on a closure that may never come.

You will have to learn to walk away and heal from unspoken apologies.

You will have to learn to heal for a long time over something that took seconds to break you.

You will have to let things go - the guilt that was never yours and a past you can never change.

You will have to learn to handle the violence and allow yourself to become gentle, despite the hands that have mishandled you.

You will have to allow yourself to feel the sadness, pain and hurt to feel the happiness that will heal every part of you.

June 2019

You will be allowed to change. It will be a part of life.

You will be allowed to wake up any day and decide to change your aesthetic.

You will be allowed to change your hairstyle, your clothing, your music taste, the way you speak, your opinions and any other aspect that you will find yourself growing out of.

You will interact with various people, and you will constantly be learning.

It will be a day-by-day process and you are allowed to change as you grow.

You are a diverse, multifaceted individual. Do not subscribe to others' perception of who they will want you to be. It will be your life and you will be allowed to grow how you see fit.

September 2019

You will get there.

You will get to the place you would have desired the most.

You will finally feel through the emotions you longed to experience, and those you would have thought were out of your reach.

You will get to a place of knowing yourself instead of allowing them to define you.

You will get there.

Do not be mistaken and think that you will get there so easily.

There will be moments you will break, and you will have to pick yourself up.

There will be moments that will shatter you to the core and you will be left questioning if the pain would have been worth it.

It will not be easy, but I assure you, it will be worth it.

You will get there.

The hardest decision you will ever have to make is
deciding between who you are
and who they want you to be

December 2019

You will have to heal what you will never be at fault for breaking.

You will have to endure sleepless nights, blurred days and the pain that will come with healing.

You will have to break the trauma bonds you will form and establish meaningful, authentic relationships.

You will have to learn the importance of boundaries.

There are people who should not have the privilege of having access to the healed you.

Do not take their jeers and ridicule to heart and break down your walls.

You will be more delicate, and you will have to curate an honest space with worthy people who will also protect your energy.

Choose your circle wisely and understand that not everyone who will want to stay, would have been meant to stay.

March 2020

Heartbreak will be inescapable and inevitable.
Partners will not be the only ones who break your heart.
Fathers will sometimes be the first to break their daughters' hearts.
Or perhaps it will be the mother or a sibling.
Platonic heartbreaks will resonate with you the most.
No matter the heartbreak, do not allow them to change you into who you are not.
Someone cold, dark.
You will learn and you will come to realize you can still love.
And still be able to have control over who you share your heart with.
You will learn to not allow them to take advantage of your kindness.
Choose wisely and love boldly.

June 2020

There are times you will not be able to recognize the person in the mirror
It will not be the prominent bags under your eyes
Or the slight frown lines that will decorate your face
It will be your eyes
The eyes tell more truth than the lips ever will
In them, you will become unrecognizable
Your lips will whisper “I’m fine,”
While your eyes scream for help
Your lips will whisper “It’s okay,”
While your eyes bleed hurt
It will be times like this that you will be torn
Between the idea of getting better and the idea of accepting the storm
That has made itself home
The answer all lies in the window of the eyes

September 2020

It will pass.
Whatever it is you feel like you will never heal from,
It will pass.
Whatever it is you feel like you will never get over,
It will pass.
Do not make the mistake of being hung up on miniscule things forever
Allow yourself to feel through the emotions for some time
It will be the only human thing to do
But believe me when I tell you, it will pass
Your chest will be burdened for some time and the emptiness will make itself at home
But as time progresses, so will you
And how pleasant it will be to look back weeks, months, or years ahead
And realize that none of it would have ever mattered.

December 2020

The last thing I will tell you is that it gets better
It will not get better right away - it is like a wave
You will have highs and lows
At times, you will be swept off your feet
At times, you will feel your head submerged in water
Even in times where you will want to give up
You will need to fight
There is a young woman out there who will be waiting to tell her story
That young women will be you
Your story will be others' survival guide
Even though you feel like you cannot make it
You will

You always will.

You should not allow them to have you questioning them why -

"Why am I not enough?"

My Darling,

You will not be at fault for what they will fail to see.

www.ingramcontent.com/pod-product-compliance
Ingram Content Group UK Ltd.
Pitfield, Milton Keynes, MK11 3LW, UK
UKHW021934190726
13853UKWH00004B/1441

9 798439 263363